Modelling Figures in Clay

Simple Animals "2".

Modelling Figures in Clay. Volume "2"

Simple Animals "2".

Introduction.

This is the second volume in our **"Clay Modelling Series"**.

In this project book we bridge the gap between the skills learned in Simple Animals Volume 1 and the more advanced skills in the **Upright Animals** project book.

The six projects in this book are designed to reinforce and expand upon the skills in the first volume.

We still use the simple shapes to which students can easily relate and templates are introduced to incorporate an element of measurement to the exercises. Templates also ensure that the models are made to the correct proportions.

Introduction of limbs and paws takes us away from the very basic concept of animal shapes and encourages students to think about the real world. For instance the ladybird from volume 1 is made using the same techniques as the tortoise in this volume. The ladybird is simply a half ball with a head whereas the tortoise is the same basic shape with a head, tail and legs attached.

The most important information in these project books is the "**Worksheet**".

Repeated use of the projects will build and reinforce the basic clay modelling skills of cutting, shaping and joining together pieces of clay and as I say the worksheet becomes all important, the picture on the sheet shows the finished product complete with shape, form and finishing details. Clay weights and templates help to keep the models in the correct proportions, the templates add **measurements** to the exercise and the finishing detail allow a degree of **self expression** to be used.

Preparation.

The Worksheet should be made available to each work group to allow them access to the templates, we have found that one sheet to four children is a good balance.

As the sheet can come into contact with wet clay it is recommended that the master is copied and each sheet is sleeved or laminated to avoid clay smudges. Once the sheets are covered they can be kept for repeated sessions and become a school resource.

When working with groups the clay should be prepared prior to the session. In fact the weighing and preparation could be used to give students practice in counting and weighing.

Preparation consists of weighing out the pieces and sealing the clay, for a specific purpose, in a plastic bag to keep it moist.

Identify the contents of each plastic bag using an indelible marker pen to add words or initials describing the intended use of the clay pieces in the bag. For example "h" on the bag could denote that the pieces in that bag were meant to be used for making the head.

Enjoy Your Clay Modelling.

Clay Modelling Tools.

All the tools can be bought in craft or hobby shops or you can produce cheap alternatives which are just as good and in some cases better and more suitable for use in schools.

Modelling tools shown are the simple tools needed for sculpting small models, most thumb pots and most coil pots.

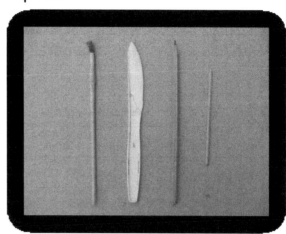

The paint brush is chosen for its stiff bristles which allow you to rough up the clay to help with cross hatching or obviate the need for cross hatching in some circumstances.

Plastic knives with the serrated edges trimmed using scissors and sharpened on sand paper are a cheap alternative to a potter's fettling knife and more suitable for use by young children. They are used primarily for cutting lengths of clay but can be used as a spatula to smooth joints between pieces of clay.

Pencils or pointed sticks, shown in the picture, are used for adding details such as eyes or hair to models or drawing patterns and designs on pots of all descriptions. The pointed stick shown was made from 3mm thick skewers used in cooking Kebabs. Cut the skewer to the length you need, I got three from one skewer, sharpen one end and round off the other end using sand paper.

The work surface shown is made from 4mm thick, three ply or MDF sheet and is 20cm x30cm.

These tools represent a one off purchase as a central resource for a school to be used by any class as required.

General Pottery Notes.

Keystones to bonding clay.

Why do we recommend working in a particular **sequence**?

We generally start with the largest piece first for two particular reasons.

Firstly to act as a base or platform on which to assemble the smaller pieces.

Secondly when bonding two pieces of clay both pieces need to be moist, or of the same consistency the first piece will be in use for the longer period and will to retain moisture until the smaller pieces are added.

Important notes found in each project.

*The creation of **slip** is an important part of joining together two pieces of clay. The water from the brush is rubbed firmly into the clay surface until it turns light grey*

***Crosshatching** is one of the keys to joining two pieces of clay. It consists of the scoring the pieces in the areas to be joined. Use the point of the knife to mark clay.*

*The use of **pressure** is essential in successfully joining two pieces of clay when used in conjunction with crosshatching and slip.*

See our "Tutorial on successful clay modelling or how to make the bits stick together".

Available from www.bmpotterycrafts.co.uk

Modelling figures in clay.

Simple Animals "2".

Contents.

1. Round Pig.

2. Penguin.

3. Dog.

4. Tortoise

5. Rabbit.

6. Smiling Cat.

B & M Potterycrafts.

Modelling Figures in Clay.

Make A Round Pig.

B & M POTTERYCRAFTS.

Make a Round Pig.

CONTENTS AND SEQUENCE.

ROLL A BALL FOR THE BODY.

MAKE AND FIT THE SNOUT.

MAKE EYES MOUTH AND NOSE.

MAKE AND FIT THE EARS.

MAKE AND FIT THE LEGS.

MAKE AND FIT THE TAIL.

MAKE AND FIT THE BASE.

MAKE A PIG WORKSHEET.

MAKE A ROUND PIG.

Roll a ball for the body.

Roll the clay between the palms of your hands, exerting sufficient force to remove any lumps or bumps. Don't be tempted to take the easy route to smooth the clay by

rolling it on the wooden work surface as this removes moisture from the clay and could make it too hard for modelling. Any creases or cracks can be smoothed using the fingers.

Continue to roll the clay until the surface is smooth and the clay is the desired shape ie a ball shape.

Make and fit the snout.

Take the clay between the palms of your hand rolling the clay until you form a smooth ball. Flatten the ball slightly by squashing it on the palm of one hand with the thumb of the other hand.

Crosshatch a spot on the body and one side of the snout using the point of your knife to score the clay with a' **#'** mark to cover the area of the snout. Use the paint brush and water to create **slip** by rubbing the brush and water firmly into the crosshatch marks on both the snout and the body. Finally **press** the snout firmly onto the body.

*The creation of **slip** is an important part of joining together two pieces of clay. The water from the brush is rubbed firmly into the clay surface until it turns light grey this is the slip and act as our glue.*

Crosshatching is one of the keys to joining two pieces of clay. It consists of scoring the pieces in the areas to be joined. Use the point of the knife to score clay.

*The use of **pressure** is essential in successfully joining two pieces of clay when used in conjunction with crosshatching and slip.*

Make eyes, mouth and nose.

Use the pointed stick to make the pig's eyes and nostrils

 pressing the point into the clay to make clear holes. Next cut the mouth into the snout using the edge of the knife as shown in the picture.

Support the body in one hand whilst adding the details.

Make and fit the ears.

To make the ears first roll the clay into a short sausage, mark the middle and then cut it in half, roll the two pieces into two small balls and squash them in the palm of one hand with the thumb of the other hand.

Use the paint brush and water firmly rubbing the brush into the surface of the clay to make two patches of slip above the eyes where the ears are to fit. Also make slip on one side of each ear in the places where the ears will fix to the head.

Firmly press each ear into the patches of slip in the positions indicated in the picture. Note that the tops of the ears are level with the pig's back to make it easier for the pig to lie on his back while his legs are attached.

Make and fit the legs.

Take the clay in the palms of your hands and roll it onto a sausage shape, try to maintain a uniform thickness along the length of the sausage shape to give you legs of an even thickness. Check the length against the template and

finally tidy up the ends by tapping the sausage shape on the work surface.

In order to make four legs of the same length first mark the sausage shape in the centre with your knife, when you are satisfied that the mark is in the centre cut the sausage

shape cleanly in half. Repeat this process with the two pieces created, mark the centres, check the position of the marks and finally cut the pieces in half.

Reshape the legs into cylindrical forms before attaching them to the pig.

To fit the legs lay the pig on his back supported on his ears, make four patches of slip with the brush and water, one at each corner. Make slip on one end of each leg and press them firmly into place.

Stand the pig on his trotters, if necessary make adjustments to the lengths to make him stand correctly.

Make and fit the tail.

Roll the clay into a thin sausage shape to the length shown on the worksheet.

Use the brush and water to make a patch of slip at the back of the pig and make slip along the whole length of the tail to make it soft and pliable.

Press one end of the tail into the patch of slip leaving the tail standing erect then curl the tail with fingers and thumb and press the curly tail into the patch of slip.

Make and fit a base.

If you wish to make the model more stable and to add more skills to the modelling exercise the following paragraph will provide the information.

 The first thing we have to do to make the base is to roll the clay into a smooth ball.

Take the ball in the palm of one hand and squash it flat with the other hand.

We need to make the base flat and large enough for the pig to stand on, not too big or the base will be too thin.

Having made the base to the correct size create four patches of slip with the brush and water on the base where the pig will stand. Make slip on the end of each leg, place the pig on the base with the ends of the legs in the patches of slip and fix it by pressing each leg firmly into place, don't press the pig as you will squash the legs.

Clay.

Body.   80 grams.

Nose.   4 grams.

Ears.   4 grams.

Legs.   15 grams. | | | | | 7 cms.

Tail.   1 gram.

Base.   40 grams.

B & M Potterycrafts.

Modelling Figures in Clay.

Make a Penguin.

B & M Potterycrafts.

Make a Penguin.

Contents and sequence.

Make the body.

Make and fit the head.

Make and fit the feet.

Make and fit the tail.

Make and fit the wings.

Make and fit the beak.

Decorate and detail the model.

Make a penguin worksheet.

Make a Penguin.

Roll a ball.

Start the process by gently squeezing the rough clay in one hand to remove the largest bumps, carry on the process of making a round smooth ball by rolling the clay between the palms of your hands, exerting sufficient force to remove any remaining lumps or bumps.

If there are any cracks on the surface smooth out these cracks by applying pressure from a finger tip, after the smoothing re-roll the clay to ensure that the surface is still smooth. Repeat this process until you achieve a ball with a smooth surface,

Don't be tempted to take the easy route to smooth the clay by rolling it on the wooden work surface as this removes moisture from the clay and could make it too hard for modelling.

Make an egg shape.

Take the clay ball between the palms of your hands and roll it into an egg shape. Roll the clay backwards and forwards across your palms exerting sufficient pressure to form the egg shape.

Once again don't be tempted to roll the clay on a hard surface as this will give a less rounded finish to the oval shape.

The best way is to roll the clay a few times, check the shape then roll it a bit more, keep rolling and checking until you get the shape that you need. Complete the shape by rounding off the ends of the egg shape with your fingers.

Head to body.

Start by rolling the clay into a smooth ball and stand the

body on one end .To attach the head to the body we need to make **crosshatch** marks and create **slip**. With the point of the plastic knife score '**#**' on the top of the body

and on the head where it is to be joined to the body. Dip the brush in water and firmly rub the brush and water across the '#' marks, the area will turn a lighter shade of grey, this material is **slip**. Finally **press** the head and body firmly together.

*The creation of **slip** is an important part of joining together two pieces of clay. The water from the brush is rubbed firmly into the clay surface until it turns light grey*

***Crosshatching** is one of the keys to joining two pieces of clay. It consists of the scoring the pieces in the areas to be joined. Use the point of the knife to mark clay.*

*The use of **pressure** is essential in successfully joining two pieces of clay when used in conjunction with crosshatching and slip.*

Make and fit the feet.

First roll the clay into a smooth ball and then roll the ball

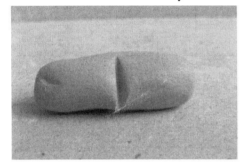 across the palms of your hands with slight pressure applied to form a short sausage shape cut this in half to make the feet. Mark the sausage shape as shown then cut it in half when you are satisfied that the mark is in the middle.

Use the brush and water to form slip in two patches where the feet are to fit, make slip on the feet where they have

been cut and press the feet into place smoothing the joint underneath the body to strengthen it. Penguins have flat feet so after assembly slightly squash the feet and flatten them a little with your finger.

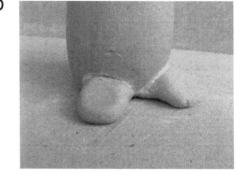

Make and fit the tail.

To make the tail the clay must first be rolled into a ball.
Roll one edge of the ball across the
palm of one hand using one finger
this method of rolling will produce a
short cone shape, when the cone is
the required length flatten the
thick end on the work surface.

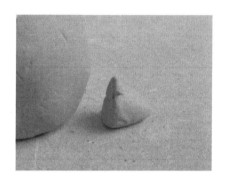

Create slip on the flattened end of the tail and also on the
penguin where the tail will fit, press the tail firmly into
place. When the tail is firmly in place press the penguin
slightly forward against the feet to make it lean forwards a
little.

Make and fit the wings.

Penguins' wings have more or less
evolved into flippers and this is how
they are used when the penguins
are swimming, in fact they look as
though they are flying under water.
The wings are short and stiff so we
need to make them quite thick.

To start making the wings roll the clay into a ball then roll
the ball into a sausage to the length shown on the
worksheet. Form the ends of the sausage into a double cone
shape by rolling the ends simultaneously between the thumb

and finger of both hands. Squash the double cone slightly with your thumb then cut the flattened piece in half to make

the wings Create slip on the body where the wings are to fit and on the wing where it will touch the body.

Press the wings firmly into place and smooth the tops to form them to the body.

Make and fit the beak.

Start the beak by rolling the clay into a ball and then into a

cone shape between the index finger and thumb of the hand. Flatten the thick end on the work surface. Create slip at the front of the head and on the thick end of the beak then press the beak into place.

Apply details.

Use the point of the wooden stick to make two holes for the penguin's eyes.

Complete the decoration by drawing a line round the front of the penguin where his white shirt will show. Also use the point of the knife to indicate claws and the sides of the beak.

B & M Potterycrafts.

Make a penguin worksheet.

Clay.

Body.	80grams.
Head.	15grams.
Wings.	5grams.
Tail.	3grams.
Feet.	4grams.
Beak.	1gram.

Scale.

Copy to this scale.   5 cms.

B & M Potterycrafts.

Modelling Figures in Clay.

Make a Dog.

B & M Potterycrafts.

Make a Dog.

Contents and sequence.

Make the body.

Make and fit the head.

Make and fit the legs.

Make and fit the tail.

Make and fit the ears.

Create the dog's features.

Make a dog worksheet.

B & M Potterycrafts.

Make a Dog.

Make the dog's body.

We always start making our figures with the most bulky piece of clay, as this piece will not dry and will stay pliable for longer, in this case it is the body.

The body in this model is an oval shape with a flattened

surface underneath.

Start by rolling the clay into a smooth ball between the palms of your hands, applying sufficient pressure to remove any lumps or

bumps from the clay, check the surface for lines or cracks and remove these with pressure from your finger, smooth the surface.

Finish off the ball with a final series of rolling movements in your hands.

We have now to change the ball shape into an egg shape which is done by rolling the ball between your hands across

your palms with enough pressure to create the oval or egg shape, continue rolling until you get the shape in the picture.

Use your fingers and thumbs to model the ends of the egg shape to make the ends rounded.

Finally tap one side of the egg shape on your work surface to make a flat area which forms the underside of the body to which we can attach the legs.

Make and fit the head.

In this version of a dog the head is made of two pieces, a ball shape for the dome of the head and a short cylinder shape for the muzzle.

Start by rolling the first piece into a smooth ball. Roll the clay between the palms of your hands with enough pressure to form the ball.

With the second piece form a second ball from which to make the muzzle. Throw the ball firmly against your work surface which makes it into a half- ball tap the rounded part on the table to make the shape shown in the picture, finally join the two pieces with slip.

Check the worksheet to determine the position of the head, it sits on the top of the body overhanging what will become the front of the dog.

With the point of your knife crosshatch the body and underneath the head in the position shown, **crosshatching** in this case can be done by scoring a simple hash '**#**' mark.

With your brush and water create slip by rubbing the water on the brush firmly across the crosshatch marks to make the pieces wet and sticky, this sticky material is called **slip** and forms our glue.

The first picture demonstrates that we have made slip on the body covering the crosshatching and slip has not yet

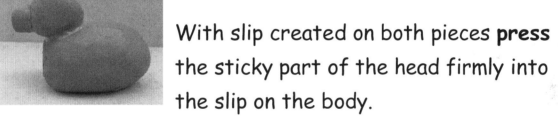

been created on the head.

With slip created on both pieces **press** the sticky part of the head firmly into the slip on the body.

The creation of **slip** is an important part of joining together two pieces of clay. The water from the brush is rubbed firmly into the clay surface until it turns light grey this is the slip and acts as our glue.

Crosshatching is one of the keys to joining two pieces of clay. It consists of the scoring the pieces in the areas to be joined. Use the point of the knife to score the clay.

The use of **pressure** is essential in successfully joining two pieces of clay when used in conjunction with crosshatching and slip.

Make and fit the legs.

Creating the legs involves first making a sausage shape and cutting this into four equal lengths to form the legs, and the fitting by making slip on the body and on the legs and pressing the legs to the body.

First roll the clay into a smooth ball in the palms of your hands then roll the ball into a sausage shape to the length shown on the template, it is important that you give the sausage shape a uniform thickness along the length.

The system adopted by B & M Potterycrafts to ensure that we make four identical legs is as follows.

Use your knife to make a mark in the centre of the sausage. When you are happy that you have marked the centre mark the centre of the two ends of the sausage shape. This time, having checked that the marks are central you cut the sausage on the marks. Press your knife through the clay try not to deform the round shape of the legs. Check that the legs are of equal length and adjust the lengths if necessary, arrange the legs as shown in the picture.

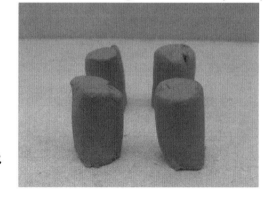

Begin fitting the legs by laying your model on it's side with the underside towards you so that you can see where the legs are fitted.

Make a patch of slip at each corner of the underside of the dog and make slip on one end of the first leg, press this leg firmly into a patch of slip at one corner. Repeat this sequence with the other three legs until you get the result shown in the picture of the dog on it's side. Your dog should now stand with all four legs touching the work surface, adjust any leg that isn't quite in position.

Make and fit the tail.

Assembling the tail consists of making a short sausage or jelly bean shape and fixing it to the back of the dog's body.

Start by rolling the piece of clay into a ball and then give it two rolls in across the palm with one finger to make a small jelly bean shape. Refer to the photograph for details of position and make a small patch of slip where the tail will fit.

Add slip on one half of the tail and press this half into the patch of slip on the body. Finally smooth the contact point with the tip of your finger to make a solid joint.

Make and fit the ears.

The dog's ears consist of a squashed sausage shape, cut in half and attached by slip and pressure to the dog's head.

Start by rolling the clay into a sausage shape the length shown on the template.

Take the sausage between the thumbs and first finger of both hands and flatten each side a little creating the shape shown.

Cut this shape in half with your knife to make the ears.

The dog's ears are situated at each side of the head slightly towards the back of the head.

Make slip with water and the brush at the side and back of the head and at the ends of the ears where they have been cut in half.

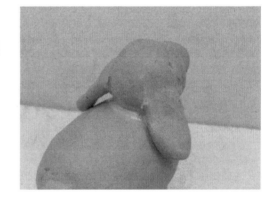

Press each ear firmly in place on the underside of the head at each side and touching the side of the body. Add a little slip where the ears touch the body to make a more stable joint.

Create the dog's features.

This final part of the exercise adds a nose, eyes, mouth and claws to our completed model.

Refer to the worksheet picture to give the positioning and shape of the final details.

Use the pointed stick to make the eyes, pushing the stick firmly into the head to give clear eyes.

Roll a tiny piece of clay into a ball and fix the ball firmly onto the top of the end of the muzzle.

Use the sharp point of the knife to carefully form the mouth. First make the single vertical line up to the nose by

simply pushing the point into the muzzle. Turn the knife point at an angle and again press the point into the muzzle, turn the blade again to form the upside down 'v'. Finally make the two side presses to form the sides of the mouth. With the pointed stick make a series of dots at each side of the muzzle to represent whiskers.

Last but not least make marks at the end of each front leg with the point of the knife to make the dog's claws.

B & M Potterycrafts.

Make a Dog. Worksheet.

Clay.

Body. 80 grams.

Head. 15 grams.

Muzzle 2grams.

Legs.   16 grams. | | | | | 7cms.

Tail.   1 gram.

Ears.   3 grams. | | |

B & M Potterycrafts.

Modelling Figures in Clay.

Make a Tortoise.

B & M Potterycrafts.

Make a Tortoise.

Contents and sequence.

Make the body.

Make and fit the head.

Make and fit the legs.

Make and fit the tail.

Decorate and detail the model.

Make a tortoise worksheet.

Make a Tortoise.

Make the body.

The first stage in making the body for the tortoise is to roll the piece of clay into a smooth ball.

Take the clay between the palms of your hands making a

shallow cup with the palm of the hand containing the clay and placing the other hand on top of the clay. Start the preparation with the upper hand rolling the piece around and around the cup.

Exert enough pressure to remove any lumps and bumps in the clay, turn the piece around occasionally continuing the rolling until you have created a round, smooth ball of clay. Remove any cracks or creases from the clay by gentle smoothing pressure from a finger and roll the clay again to complete the smooth surface. This is important because the cracks and creases are weak points in the shape and could

spoil your model. Do not be tempted to roll the clay on your absorbent work surface because you will remove moisture from the clay and make it too dry and hard to shape.

The second stage in making the body is to change the ball shape into a half ball shape, you can challenge students into suggesting how the half ball is achieved, cutting and squashing are favourite answers but the simple method is to throw the clay firmly **once** onto the work surface.

Clear your tools from the work-surface, take the ball between the fingers of your throwing hand, make several practice movements towards the surface and finally throw the ball onto the surface with sufficient force to deform it into the half ball shape needed.

Make and fit the head.

The small piece of clay to make the head is first rolled into a smooth ball then placed in the palm of one hand and rolled firmly across the palm with the other hand, one or two rolls should make the length and shape shown in the picture, check the length  by measuring the head against the template on the worksheet.

Dip the brush into the water and rub the brush around the point where the head is to be fitted, the brush and water produce a material called **slip** which acts as our glue.

Note. In all cases of joining two pieces of clay together the creation of slip accompanied by the application of pressure and a sliding or twisting motion between the parts to be joined is essential to create a secure joint.

 Create slip on one end of the head and firmly press and slightly twist the end of the head with slip on it into the patch of slip on the body.

Check the still photo for this step and slightly tilt the head upwards as shown in the photo.

Make and fit legs.

Making the legs starts with rolling the piece of clay into a sausage shape to the length of the template shown on the worksheet.

Roll the clay between your palms trying to keep the same

thickness along the full length. To achieve a uniform thickness of the sausage shape I have found that if you roll the clay a few times, stop and check the length against the

template and recheck the shape. If the sausage shape is a bit thick in places concentrate on these thick places on the next roll. Check the length against the template and repeat this process until you achieve the desired length.

Cutting the sausage shape into four equal lengths is the next challenge, I have found that the easiest and most accurate way is to mark the clay in the centre with your plastic knife and only cut it in half when you are satisfied that the mark is in the centre.

Repeat this process on the two pieces created, again only cut the clay when you are satisfied that the marks are in the centre. Using this method should give you four legs of equal length and thickness.

To complete the preparation of each leg prior to fixing the legs to the tortoise each leg is rolled gently between the palms of your hands to round off the sharp uneven edges created with cutting the clay. As shown in the still photo.

Fixing the legs to the body involves first creating four patches of slip on the underside of the tortoise.

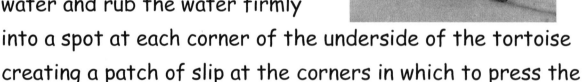

Turn the tortoise over and lay it on the shell, dip your brush in the water and rub the water firmly into a spot at each corner of the underside of the tortoise creating a patch of slip at the corners in which to press the legs.

The next step is to brush water firmly onto each leg along half the length of the leg and press the area of leg containing slip firmly into a patch of slip on the body, repeat this with the other legs positioning each one as shown on the still photo.

After positioning the legs as shown in the photo press the end of each leg into the body to strengthen the bond between legs and body.

Make and fit the tail.

The tail for the tortoise is first made by rolling the clay into a smooth ball then forming the ball into a cone shape.

The simplest way to achieve a small cone is to roll one side of the ball between the thumb and fingers of the hand with sufficient pressure to create a short point, complete the 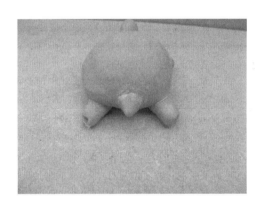 exercise by pressing the thick end of the piece onto the work surface to flatten it.

Make a small patch of slip on the shell at the rear end of the tortoise and on the flattened portion of the cone shape. Finally press the tail firmly into place on the model.

Decorate and detail the model.

Details for the head consist of making the eyes and the mouth.

Make two holes for the eyes with the pointed stick and push the sharp edge of the plastic knife into the front of the

head to create the mouth, check the photo for positioning of these features.

Use the point of the knife to make claws in the two front legs and the pointed stick to draw circles in a pattern on the shell of the tortoise.

B & M Potterycrafts.

Tortoise Worksheet.

Clay.

Body. 80grams.

Head. 5grams.

Legs. 12grams.

Tail. 1gram

8 cms.

B & M Potterycrafts.

Modelling Figures in Clay.

Make a Rabbit.

B & M Potterycrafts.

Make a Rabbit.

Contents and sequence.

Make the body.

Make and fit the head.

Make and fit the front paws.

Make and fit the back legs.

Make and fit the tail.

Make and fit the ears.

Create the rabbit's features.

Make a rabbit worksheet.

B & M Potterycrafts.

Make a Rabbit.

Roll a ball.

Roll the clay between the palms of your hands, exerting

sufficient force to remove any lumps or bumps. Don't be tempted to take the easy route to smooth the clay by rolling it on the wooden work surface as this removes moisture from the clay and could make it too hard for modelling. Any creases or cracks can be smoothed using the fingers. Continue to roll the clay until the surface is smooth and the clay is the desired shape, that is a ball shape.

Make an egg shape.

Take the clay ball between the palms of your hands and roll it into an egg shape. Roll the clay backwards and forwards across your palms exerting sufficient pressure to form the

egg shape. The best way is to roll the clay a few times, check the shape then roll it a bit more, keep rolling and checking until you get the shape that you need. Complete the shape

by rounding off the ends of the egg with your fingers.

One final touch is to slightly flatten the underside of the rabbit's body by gently tapping the clay on the work surface until you achieve the shape shown in the still photo. This action makes it more stable and creates an edge to which the feet can be attached.

Make and fit the head.

Roll the clay into a smooth ball in the palms of your hands,

when the ball is prepared give it two more rolls across your palms applying sufficient pressure to deform the clay and to create a pointed egg shape as shown in the picture.

With the point of the knife scratch the '**#**' sign on the head and on the body where the head is going to fit. This is called **crosshatching.** These marks should be deep enough to break the surface of the clay as demonstrated in the

picture. Dip the brush in water and rub the brush firmly across the crosshatch marks to create **slip,** this helps the clay bond together.

Press the head and body firmly together to fix the head, as you apply the pressure slide the two pieces slightly together these actions combine to make a firm bond between the two surfaces.

The creation of *slip* is an important part of joining together two pieces of clay. The water from the brush is rubbed firmly into the clay surface until it turns light grey

Crosshatching is one of the keys to joining two pieces of clay. It consists of the scoring the pieces in the areas to be joined. Use the point of the knife to mark clay.

The use of *pressure* is essential in successfully joining two pieces of clay when used in conjunction with crosshatching and slip.

Make and fit the front paws.

The making the front paws is simply to roll the clay into a smooth ball, mark the centre of the ball with your knife, check that the mark is in the centre and cut it in half.

Rabbits generally sit with their front paws at the front of the body not touching each other but set apart. Position the front paws as shown in the picture directly in front of the body. Use the brush and water to create slip on the body and the paws then press the paws firmly into position and smooth the underside of the joint with the fingers to make the joint stronger.

Make and fit the back legs.

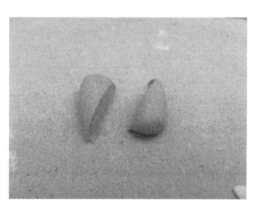

Making and fitting the back legs requires a different technique to be adopted from that used when fitting of the front paws. First roll the clay into a ball then into a sausage shape to the length indicated on the template. Mark the sausage shape diagonally and cut the clay at an angle as shown in the picture.

Cutting the clay at an angle allows the legs to stick out from each side of the body at a realistic angle.

Create slip with the brush and water on both the legs and body and press the legs firmly into place, as you press the legs into the body rub the pieces together, pressing into the slip helps the joints to bond together.

Make and fit the tail.

Roll the small piece of clay into a smooth ball in the palms of
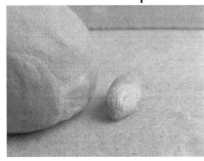
your hands. Having formed the ball shape roll the ball between your palms forming the elongated oval shape shown in the picture. With the brush and water make slip on one side of the tail covering half the surface, make a corresponding patch of slip on the back of the rabbit's body then firmly press

the tail into place as shown in the
picture. Complete the process by
applying pressure and smoothing
the joint on the body with your
fingers, position the tail slightly
away from the body as shown.
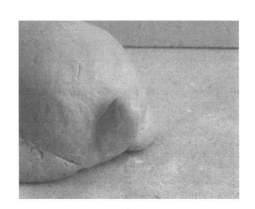

Make and fit the ears.

Start by rolling the clay into a smooth ball then roll it into a
sausage shape to the length shown on the worksheet.

When rolling the sausage shape try to keep the same
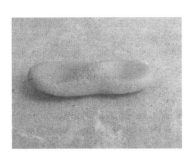
thickness along the full length of the sausage shape.

Rabbit's ears are not rounded but overall they are flat so use pressure from your thumb to slightly squash the sausage at each end to create the shape shown. Use the knife to cut this strip of clay in half to form the two ears.

With water and the brush make slip on the back of the head and on the ears where they have been cut. Press the ears firmly onto the head as shown in the picture.

Create the rabbit's features.

These features are the eyes, mouth nose and claws and these are applied as follows, with the little wooden stick make two holes for the eyes, remembering that rabbit's eyes are at the side of the head.

The mouth and nose are made at the same time by pressing the edge of the knife twice at the front of the head to form an 'X'. Pressing the knife into the clay rather than drawing the cross has the effect of pushing up the clay at each side and forming the nose at the same time.

B & M Potterycrafts.

Worksheet.

Make a Rabbit.

Clay and Sequence.

Body.   80 grams.

Head.   10 grams.

Front Paws.   2 grams.

Back legs.   5 grams.

Tail.   1 gram.

Ears.   5 grams.   ▭

Scale.   ▭ 4 cms.

Important. Copy this sheet to scale.

B & M Potterycrafts.

Make a Smiling Cat.

B & M Potterycrafts.

Make a Smiling Cat.

Sequence and contents.

Roll a ball.

Make an egg shape.

Make and fit the head.

Make and fit front paws.

Make and fit the back legs.

Make and fit tail.

Make and fit the ears.

Add finishing touches.

Worksheet, Make a smiling cat.

B & M Potterycrafts

Make a smiling cat.

Roll a ball.

Roll the clay between the palms of your hands, exerting  sufficient force to remove any lumps or bumps. Don't be tempted to take the easy route to smooth the clay by rolling it on the wooden work surface as this removes moisture from the clay and could make it too hard for modelling. Any creases or cracks can be smoothed using the fingers. Continue to roll the clay until the surface is smooth and the clay is the desired shape ie a ball shape.

Make an egg shape.

Take the clay ball between the palms of your hands and roll it two or three times to make an egg shape. Roll the clay backwards and forwards across your palms exerting sufficient pressure to form the egg shape. The best way is to roll the clay a few times, check the shape then roll it a bit more, keep  rolling and checking until you get the shape that you need. Complete the shape by rounding off the ends of the egg with your fingers.

Make and fit the head.

Roll the clay into a smooth ball in the palms of your hands. Next action is to slightly flatten the ball, place it in the palm of your hand and pat the ball gently with the other hand to produce the shape shown in the picture.

With the point of the knife scratch the **#** sign on the head and on the body where the head is going to fit. This is called **crosshatching.** Dip the brush in water and rub the brush firmly across the crosshatch marks to create **slip,** this helps the clay bond together.

Press the head and body firmly together to fix the head.

Please note that the head appears to be at a peculiar angle, this is because the cat's head is turned to the side and seems to be attached to the side of the body.

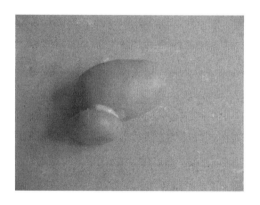

*The creation of **slip** is an important part of joining together two pieces of clay. The water from the brush is rubbed firmly into the clay surface until it turns light grey*

***Crosshatching** is one of the keys to joining pieces of clay. It consists of the scoring the pieces in the areas to be joined. Use the point of the knife to mark clay.*

*The use of **pressure** is essential in successfully joining two pieces of clay when used in conjunction with crosshatching and slip.*

Make and fit front paws.

The making the front paws is simply to roll the clay into a smooth ball, mark the centre of the ball with your knife, check that the mark is in the centre and cut it in half.

Position the front paws as shown in the picture sticking out directly in front of the body. Cats normally lie with their front paws side by side and touching so they should be

positioned as shown in the picture. Use the brush and water to create slip on the body and the paws where they were cut then press the paws firmly into position and smooth the joint with the fingers.

Make and fit the back legs.

Making the back legs for the cat prior to fitting them to

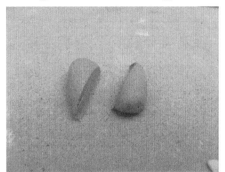

the body consists of first rolling the clay into a ball and then into a sausage shape, roll a short sausage shape check the length against the template and repeat this process until the correct length is reached. The next activity is to mark the clay diagonally and cut the clay at an angle.

The angled cut allows the legs to stick out from the body as shown in the picture.

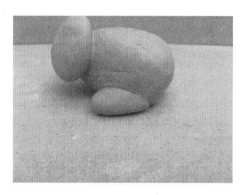

Create slip with the brush and water on the legs and on the body press each leg firmly into the slip on the body accompanying the pressure with a slight sliding motion which helps to bond the legs firmly into place.

Make and fit tail.

To make and fit the tail the clay is first rolled into a ball and then into a sausage shape to the length shown on the template.

Roll the clay into a ball then place it in the palm of your hand, use the fingers of your other hand to fashion the ball into a sausage shape by rolling with pressure across the

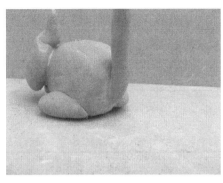

palm. After a few rolls check the length, repeat this process until you get the required length.

Use your brush and water to create a patch of slip on the body and along the length of the tail to make it flexible. Press the end of the tail firmly into the body and blend the clay joint with finger pressure. Make a patch of slip on the cat's back and on the cat's tail, form the tail as shown and press the tail into the slip on the cat's back, refer to the worksheet for the bends and the position of the tail.

Make and fit the ears.

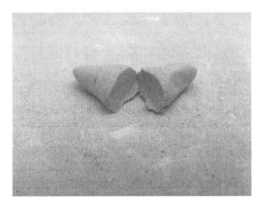

To make the ears we use the technique of rolling a double ended cone shape and cutting it in half to make the ears.

Start by rolling the clay into a ball shape, trap the ball between

the tips of both index fingers and the thumbs. With gentle pressure roll the clay backwards and forwards between the thumbs and fingers, this action will produce a double ended cone shape which when cut in half makes the pointed ears. Make slip on the head and on the ears where they were cut and press the ears into place.

This technique can be adopted in making pointed ears or horns of different lengths for several types of animals. Simply adjust the rolling to produce longer or shorter cones as required.

Add finishing touches.

Use the point of the wooden stick to make two eyes and a large grinning mouth.

Make a small ball for the cat's nose, make slip on the face and on the nose and press the nose into place.

Press the tip of the plastic knife into all four paws to simulate claws, also use the knife tip to add the cat's whiskers.

B & M POTTERYCRAFTS.

MAKE A SMILING CAT WORKSHEET.

Clay.

Body. 80 grams.

Head. 15 grams.

Paws. 3 grams.

Legs. 10 grams.

Tail. 5 grams.

Ears. 2 grams.

Nose. Small piece.

Scale.   5 cms.

Printed in Great Britain
by Amazon